JUST SOUTH OF THE RAINBOW

Barbara A. Pierce

Drawings by Antonio Dimas and the Author.

Library of Congress Control Number: 2007903282
ISBN: Hardcover 978-1-4257-7208-6
Softcover 978-1-4257-7204-8

This book was printed in the United States of America.

To order additional copies of this book, contact:
Xlibris Corporation
1-888-795-4274
www.Xlibris.com
Orders@Xlibris.com

36080

CONTENTS

The Origin of Thunder and Lightning....9
Sometimes I Wish That I Could Fly....11
An Earthquake, A Deadly Force....12
The Rainbow....13
A Rare Sky View....15
My Private Domain....17
Big Shoes To Fill....19
Granny's Medicine....21
Pile Them High In Stacks....23
A Greedy Old Fox....25
The Dishwasher....27
The Selfish King....29
Just One Little Lick....31
Hot Dogs and Baked Beans With Coleslaw....33
A Routine For Life....35
Busy Little Ants....37
A Very Good Day....38
Just To Be Cool....39
The Lion Is King....41
My Brothers Lied....43
Choose Your Words Wisely....44
Moments....45
Much The Same....46
Fishing Is Not For Me....47
Shana's Last Time At The Fair....49
Weird Things Happen On Halloween....51
A Fascination With Shoes....53
Strange Animal Sightings....55
There's A Bit Of Pirate In Me....57
Laughter Is Good For The Soul....59

Under The Big Top 61
And That Is Okay..62
An Autumn Warning...63
Another School Year 65
Making Good Choices 66
Another Fall Season...67
The Yellow Balloon 69
Music Tickles My Fancy...71
What A Situation 73
Let Them Play...75
Moonstruck...77
June Bug Days...79
Couplets..80

Dedication and Acknowledgements

This book is dedicated to the administrators Peter Ragaglia and Barbara Pisano, the faculty, the staff and the students at Columbus Elementary School in Mount Vernon, New York.

A special thanks to all of those who have continued to support my work.

The Origin of Thunder and Lightning

There are many accounts of how thunder
And lightning came about.
As for the facts being true in this one,
There's certainly room for doubt.
So the story goes,
Quiitar and Ishaar two angry, colossal, young
Rams
Together set out to destroy the worlds
Great dams.
To everyone in the universe their mission was
Clear.
Surely it was to cause panic among all the
People and promote global fear.
When the people began to voice their concerns
About what was brewing
Providence, the caretaker of the universe, heard
And immediately stopped what he was doing
To fully investigate Quiitar and Ishaar's intentions.
He arrived right in the mist of one of their loud
And riotous dissensions.
The caretaker suggested they take their battle into
The sky
Where he thought they would cool down as they
Started to fly.
Thus what a surprise to hear the heart stopping
Claps of thunder coming from on high,
Preceded by sharp flashes of blinding light
Seemingly going awry.
An all out display of unleashed fury was
Taking place for all the world to see
With horns clashing and sparks flying as
Violently as could be.
Quiitar and Ishaar were then commanded by
The Great Providence to remain forever in the
Upper tier.
Now, whenever it's thundering and lightning
It is said the rams are battling it out in the
Atmosphere.

Sometimes I Wish That I Could Fly

Sometimes I wish that I could fly
Like the birds up in the sky
Above the clouds I would soar,
Above the rainbow and then lower.
Back and forth I would go,
Around and about
Up and down, in and out
And perhaps hover for a while in
In just one spot
As the humming bird does to drink
From the flower its lot.
Then back to the open sky I would
Head
In which ever direction my fantasy
Led.

An Earthquake, A Deadly Force

The deadly force of an earthquake
Rips open the land.
Straight down the center large
Cracks expand
As the opened crust violently
Shakes.
For seconds and minutes it
Rumbles and quakes.
Waves of energy from the epicenter
Radiate and spread
In all directions for miles and miles
And miles ahead
Until the motion slowly decreases
And suddenly Earth's vigorous
Rocking ceases.

The Rainbow

The rainbow,
What a spectacular sight,
Brilliant strands of colors dispersing light
From a majestic arched canopy
Suspended far out in the atmosphere
Surrounded by an enormous sky
And clouds lingering near.
What a spectacular sight to see__
The rainbow in all of its enormity!

A Rare Sky View

Tonight, I'm lying motionless, peering up
At an awesomely beautiful sky,
Watching the soft, billowy clouds as
They meander slowly by.
What a wonderful, wonderful feeling
Witnessing mother nature so appealing!
Oh how I wish I could remain here
For a much, much longer time.
The thought of staying forever is suddenly
Quite sublime
To continue to watch a phenomenon that's
Rarely committed to view,
Nature's breathtaking sky,
A purple and lavender hue.

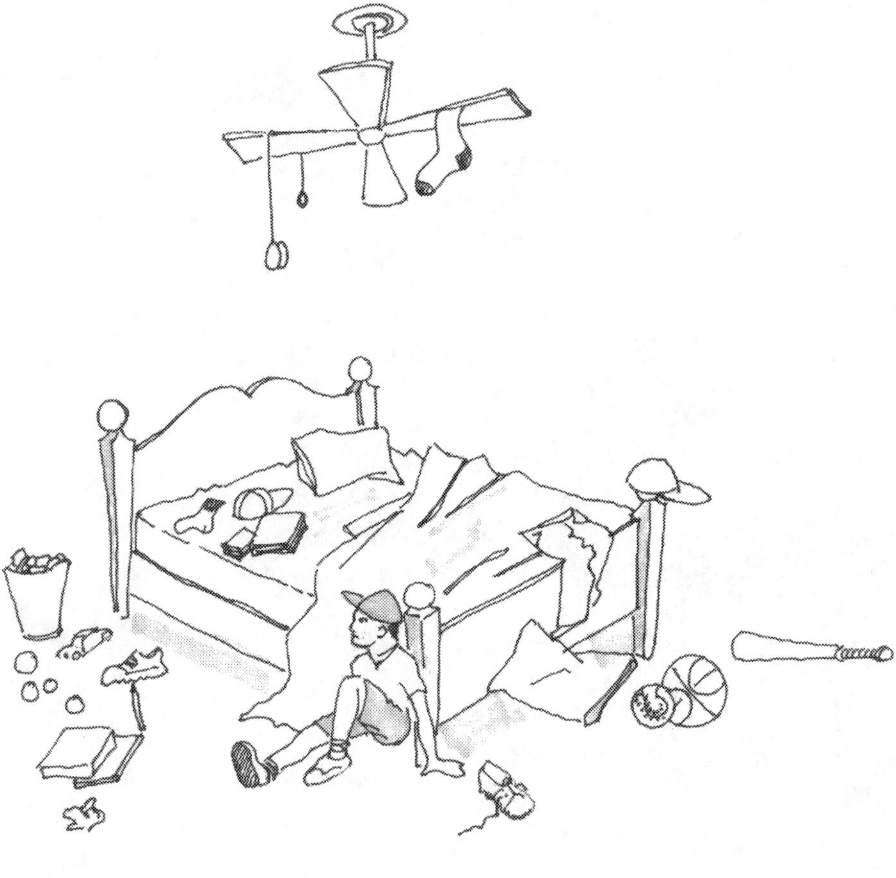

My Private Domain

My bedroom is suppose to be my own
Private domain.
A fact to my family I keep trying to
Explain.
It's the place I go to be all alone,
To do my home work, or to talk privately
On the phone.
Dad comes in often to say my room's a pigsty,
When I am trying to rest.
Gee, doesn't he know by now, that's how I
Like it best!
It feels so homey with stuff crumpled in my
Bed and in mounds on the floor,
And my pyjamas and underwear hung
Conveniently over the door.
When I'm told to clean up what they call
My mess, I know I'd better abide.
Nevertheless I'm confused, If it's my room,
When to clean it, why can't I decide?
When I get older I'll get a place and clean
Once a year.
But for now, it looks like I'm stuck in this one
Right here!

Big Shoes To Fill

When I was just a little tyke, before the age of seven
My older brother, Bill was a strong robust eleven.
How I admired his cleverness and all the things he
Was able to do.
He was not just my brother, he was my idol too.
Every time I mentioned to my family and friends that
When I grew up, I wanted to be like Bill,
Over and over I was told I had big shoes to fill.
Of course, then I did not know the meaning of such a
Phrase.
All I could do was just stare at my brother's shoes in a
Wishful kind of gaze
And hope that my feet would grow quickly to fit in Bill's
Shoes.
Little did I know then that it was just an expression that many
People use.
(The expression means that one is so good at what he or
she does that someone else will have to work very hard
to be equally as good.)

Granny's Medicine

My old granny is a very special lady.
Besides being called Nanna, she's called
Doctor Sadie.
She does so much to keep the whole family
Happy and well,
Trying to recall all the things she does, is
Impossible to tell.
She takes drastic action when anyone gets
Hurt or sick.
From a variety of old fashion remedies
She usually will pick.
Just tasting and smelling the concoctions
Make her patients gag, sputter, and spit.
But Doctor Sadie refuses to give up or
Let any of them quit.
Further instructions are to breathe deeply
And then take a swallow
And immediately after__ a long soothing nap
Should follow.
Though Granny's unpleasant doctoring
Pays off,
Everyone becomes extremely anxious
With the threat of a sneeze or the slightest
Little cough.

Pile Them High In Stacks

Pancakes, flapjacks,
Flip them, flap them,
Pile them high in stacks.
Keep them coming!
Not one,
Make it two, three, or
Four,
And maybe even more.
Dredge them with lots of
Butter and syrup a plenty.
Keep pouring the syrup,
And listen__ before you ask,
I'm not sharing any!

A Greedy Old Fox

A greedy old fox spied six plump hens
Sleeping in a box.
He gobbled, gobbled, gobbled,
Then he wobbled, wobbled, wobbled
To a flight of stairs
Up which he hobbled, hobbled, hobbled
To the top,
Then plop, plop, plop
Down the flight of stairs he toppled,
Toppled, toppled.
Such a fitting end for any greedy old fox
Who'd gobble up six plump hens sleeping
In a box.

The Dishwasher

My family needs a dishwasher, because I'm
Tired of being it!
If I had some place else to go, I think that
I would quit!
What a chore doing dishes every single day!
Very often I get the urge to throw a few away!
Dad probably wouldn't notice,
But Mom certainly would.
The reason that I wash them is because
She says I should.
Pretty soon they're going to ask what gift I
Want for my birthday.
A dishwasher__ is what I think I should say.
Yes, that's exactly what I'm going to say!

The Selfish King

King Beazel built a castle, around which he dug a moat
To avoid the constant hassle
Of finding a harbor to anchor his precious boat.
He now thought about his position in life
And realized what his home was lacking,
A lively, smart, and happy little wife.
He stopped, then asked himself if he could tolerate her
Endless yakking,
Or she, his bad manners and constant snacking?
King Beazel decided that to find out
Would be too much of a hassle,
So he chose to remain all alone in his
Big lonely castle.

Just One Little Lick

(Beware of those that refuse at first,
then change their minds.)
What's that you have, ice cream?
What flavor, Raspberry Supreme?
I don't eat ice cream, it usually
Makes me sick!
Okay, this time, just one little lick.
Oh, I'm sorry, it was sooooo—good!
I guess I ate more than I should!
Now, I really do feel sick!
I got to run home now,
Quick, quick, quick!

Hot Dogs and Baked Beans With Coleslaw

Hot dogs and baked beans with coleslaw are my
Favorite foods to eat.
So delicious, others think of them also as a great
Tasting treat!
When I grow up and become President, I plan to
Introduce a law
That parents must serve their kids once a week
Hot dogs and baked beans with coleslaw.
Perhaps, I'll make it our country's national dish,
Replacing the ever popular greasy French fries
And smelly, old fish.
Well tomorrow, I'll consider the matter some
More,
But now the table is being served with my
Favorites galore,
The meal that leaves me in splendid awe,
Hot dogs and baked beans with scrumptious
Coleslaw!

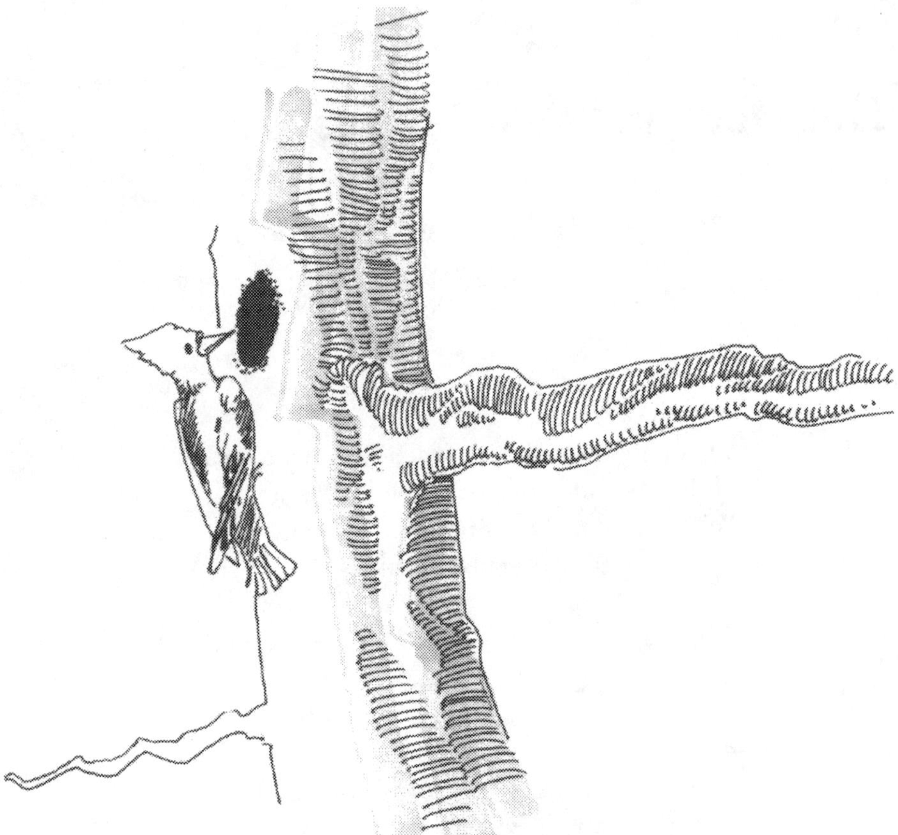

A Routine For Life

At the top of a tall tree
A woodpecker lands
Prepared to begin work
Right where he stands.
Knock-knock-knock
With his beak he starts
To pound and pound
And pound.
Knock-knock-knock
His urgency shows!
Knock-knock-knock
It grows and grows
With his preoccupation
Of building a home,
Knock-knock-knock
One of his very own
Knock-knock-knock
To house his future brood
And a brand new wife.
Knock-knock-knock
Knock-knock-knock
A routine he will follow
For the rest of his life.
Knock-knock-knock
Knock-knock-knock.

Busy Little Ants

Ants travel back and forth keeping actively busy
Without any signs of tiring or even getting dizzy.
Each ant carries loads much greater than its weight,
Continuing a pace at a consistent and steady rate.
If a load is dropped, it is retrieved quickly again,
Then the journey is resumed as per the original plan.
While some ants may appear to be on their own,
They are not really all alone.
Things are just not as they seem.
The hard working insects are part of a team
Whose goal is to provide for the colony
That thousands of them share.
Wherever there's an ant hill, there's probably
A colony there.

A Very Good Day

Today is a very good day.
There is nothing bothering me.
I am as happy as a parrot in a kapok tree.
Can't you see there is nothing bothering me!
Though not everything has turned out as
Planned,
That's life, I do understand.
Today is still a very good day.
There is nothing bothering me.
Can't you see! Can't you see!
I am as happy as a parrot in a kapok tree.

Just To Be Cool

Dear Mommie,
I know that you love me as much as I love you,
So please read my letter all the way through.
And please don't get upset with what I say.
You know when you take me to school each day,
You don't say good-bye and just walk away.
Ma, you kiss me, and hug me, and even hold my hand!
It's just so embarrassing, can you understand?
As soon as you drive off my buddies begin to chant
That I'm a little mama's boy.
They all seem to have so much fun, but for me there's no
Such joy!
And then they tell me I'm not cool.
So Mommie, please no more kissing, no more hand holding,
Or hugging in the school!
And Mom, just one thing more.
In the morning, before we reach the school's front door,
Drop me off a block away and let me walk__
Then the kids will think I'm really cool and stop their
Childish talk.

Love,
Your son, Cool Alex

P.S. Please, please think about it Mommie, please!

The Lion Is King

The mighty lion in the wild is said to be king.
Because of his fearlessness he rules everything.
The chances for the survival of other animals
Are mighty slim
When this hungry carnivore targets any one of
Them.
Though pain-staking efforts are made to avoid
His view
Still they are vulnerable, not having the slightest
Clue
About this hunter's shrewdness and Keen eyesight.
Already it's to late for the prey when it begins to take
Flight.
The relentless chase and vicious kill never take very
Long
For his precise calculations are hardly ever wrong.
Such strength and ferocious behavior ensures continued
Feasts
For the lion in the wild, the true king of beasts.

My Brothers Lied

I've always dreamed of climbing a tree.
It's easy my brothers kept telling me.
So without thinking things through,
That's what I set out to do.
But when I tried, I found out they lied.
The proof, these scratches and scrapes
All over my hide,
Especially those on my backside!

Choose Your Words Wisely

Remember, words are used to
Communicate.
So use them wisely!
Words can alienate.
Words can instill hate.
Words can be a barometer
To evaluate.
Words can cause pain and humiliate.
Words said in anger
Can never be retracted.
Words when remembered
Is a scene re-enacted.
While other words may take
Their place,
The damage done is hard to erase!
So choose your words wisely.

Moments

Our lives are but vast bundles of moments:
Moments of pleasures and moments of anguish.
Each moment has significant worth.
Some moments are very special.
Those are the moments we choose to remember.
And certainly there are those moments we wish to
Forget.
Still, there remain those redefining moments
We've not experienced yet!

Much The Same

It is said girls perspire, not sweat.
Boys sweat according to standard etiquette.
But there is irony in it all
While relatively small,
Whatever the designated name
The final outcome is much the same
Whether it is perspire or sweat
Everyone ends up miserably wet.

Fishing Is Not For Me

Fishing, many say is a wonderful sport.
"So you say!" is usually my retort.
Baiting a hook with a squirming worm,
That is truly not for me!
Fishing just isn't where I want to be.
Where is the pleasure lingering in one spot
For hours
Through the sun spikes and the sporadic rain
Showers
Waiting for the fish to bite
Sometimes until late, late into the night
Still waiting for the fish to bite?
The one and only time I ever went fishing
Left me wishing and feeling so blue.
My only catch was a rusty tin can and a soggy
Dilapidated shoe.
No—fishing is not where I want to be.
It is not the sport for me!

Cyclone

Shana's Last Time At The Fair

The last time Shana went to the fair
She got so caught up in the excitement
There
And mounted the giant roller coaster
Ride
Ignoring the warning feelings inside.
Too late, Shana asked herself if she had
Lost her mind,
While trying to reason with the operator
To leave her behind.
Again too late, she was in the loop.
Up the ramp, down the ramp she went,
Sloopity-sloop Sloopity-sloop.
When the screams began, the loudest
Came from her.
The dizzying ride became a total blur.
Besides the loud wailing, there was
Nothing she could do
But to hold on for dear life 'til the grueling
Ride was through.

Weird Things Happen On Halloween

Halloween is on its way,
Due to arrive most any day.
When it does a transformation will take place.
There'll be monster samplings and a trick or treat
Race.
As little gray bats and big black cats are being
Pursued for a witches' brew
With the help of ghosts and goblins
While other witches do what witches do,
Hunt for other special ingredients.
THAT COULD BE YOU, (Point to those listening.)
To also add to their pot of stew!
So beware of those dressed in costume
Depicting the creatures of doom
To avoid becoming a possible meal
In case one in disguise is for real.
Remember, weird things do happen
On Halloween!

SHOE
DEPOT
DC
SHOES

A Fascination With Shoes

We have such a fascination with shoes.
White shoes, red shoes, black shoes, blue shoes
All color shoes
Old shoes, new shoes
Likely bought in pairs by twos
High tops, loafers, dress shoes
Casual and sport shoes
Got the blues, buy more shoes!
Just any kind of shoes!
One really does not need a reason.
Buying shoes is always in season,
Even when we have shoes galore__
We just keep buying more and more.
What a fascination we have with shoes!

Strange Animal Sightings

A polka dot pig dancing with a hairless monkey wearing
A wig

A big gray elephant in a yellow frock with one shoe on
And one sock

A frisky featherless hen turned upside down doing a dizzying
Head spin

A parade of caterpillars traveling in twos all wearing mix—matched
High-top shoes

Penguins changing from their black and white tuxedos into flashy zoot
Suits and buttoned down spat boots

J.T., a portly purple hippopotamus driving a little yellow school bus

There's A Bit Of Pirate In Me

I'm convinced that there is a bit of pirate in me
Because in my dreams I am always at sea
Aboard big wooden vessels of an era long ago
As Captain Peg-Leg Pete with my trusted first mate,
One-Eyed Joe.
We're the most feared pirates to ever sail any distant
Waterway;
Jumping from ship to ship, plundering their bounty
And reeking havoc in anyone's path we stray.
Our many dangerous and rip-rowing adventures are
Too numerous to tell,
But in the end just like the Three Musketeers, we're
Always victorious and everything turns out well.
Now, do you see why I say that there's a bit of pirate in me?

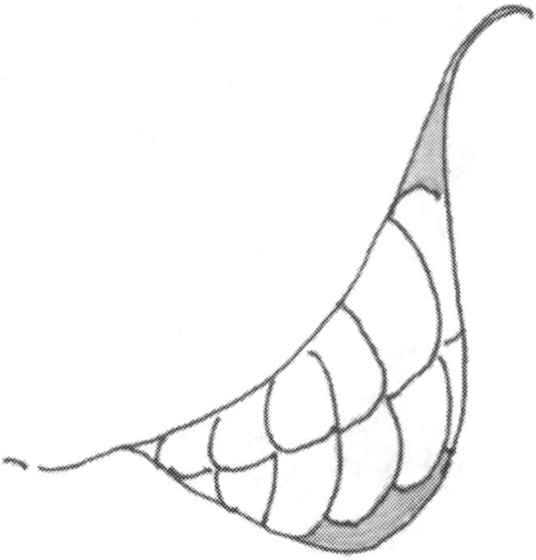

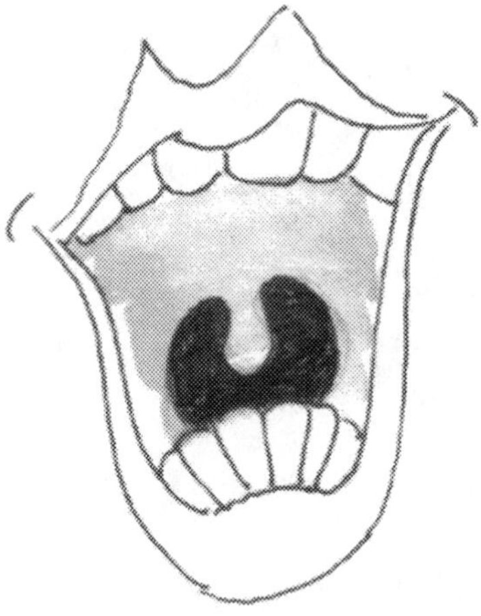

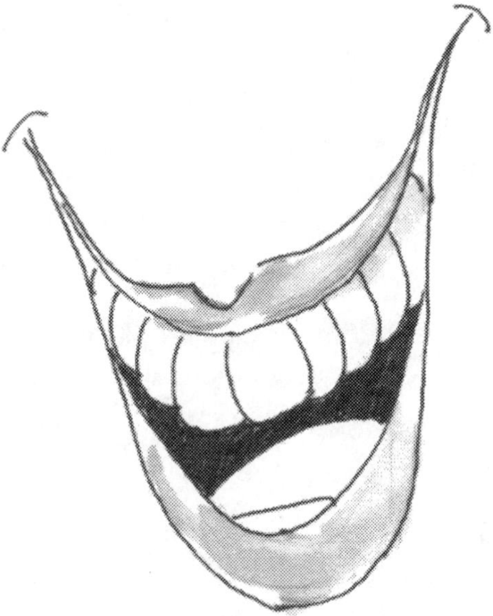

Laughter Is Good For The Soul

It is true that laughter is good for the soul.
Laughter lifts the spirit high and lightens
A heavy load
And it keeps a heart from turning cold
In the young as well as in the old.
Laughter should never be allowed to flicker out
As does the flame on a candle
Or become a forgotten thing of the past
For it encourages those sparks in one's life
To flourish and to last.

CIRCUS
WELCOME

Under The Big Top

Come and go with me under the Big Top
To join in fun and laughter that's non-stop.
There is sure to be many great surprises
And perhaps chances to win some fabulous
Prizes.
Don't be shocked to hear loud thunderous claps,
High-pitched 'wows' during intended mishaps,
And to witness hilarious gags of bumbling clowns
Wearing silly smiles or even sillier frowns
As they tumble and fumble while balancing bottles
And juggling hats.
And what a defiance of gravity by those fearless
Acrobats!
Other spell-binding acts just to name a few,
A tip-top magic show with an irresistible view,
A tottering tightrope walker, and one who eats fire,
And a human cannon ball, soon to be a high flyer.
Wait, that's not all!
Though some trainers perform admirably with animals
That are small,
There are those suspenseful acts that will touch a
Nerve or two
Because you never know what the larger ones are liable
To do.
There's the dancing black bear, elephants doing tricks,
White horses prancing about,
Trainers caged with lions and tigers acting out.
The excitement is heightened by lively music
And familiar smells that penetrate the air
Mesmerizing and energizing everyone that's there__
Under the Big Top
Where fun and laughter continue non-stop!

And That Is Okay

Are you a sore looser when you are challenged
And do not win?
Do you sit and actually pout,
Or do you just take it on the chin,
Until you have thought it all out,
Then concluding, you really do not mine,
But hope the next encounter will be your
Chance to shine?
Remember this one little thought on
Your way:
In life you will win some and you will loose
Some,
And That Is Okay!

An Autumn Warning

Autumn, the season when crops
And fruits are gathered and trees drop their
Colorful leaves
Portraying nature as the picture of splendor
And great ease.
Though Autumn dwells between Summer and
Winter: seasonal extremes,
Also called Fall, it boasts of its own particular
Weather schemes,
Generally mild temperatures influenced by
Occasional lofty winds,
Familiar warning signals to all living things
Nature sends,
That now__ it is time to begin preparations
To weather the coming season's
Harsh transformations.

Another School Year

The summer is over,
Now back to the books,
Lots of home work,
And teachers' stern looks,
Old friendships renewed,
New friendships pursued,
Another year of enlightenment,
And school days full of excitement,
Many periods of academic review
Before learning something totally
New.
Numerous assignments given,
But when left undone,
Extended days, void of all the fun.
Now officially,
Another school year has begun!

Making Good Choices

When you are asked to make choices,
Really listen to those strong inner voices.
Think pass all present distractions,
And any other interfering actions.
Good choices take time to make.
Give full consideration to all that's
At stake,
The benefits and the consequences,
Possible outcomes with harsh recompenses
Spurred on by the wrong choices.
Really listen to those strong inner voices.
Then you are bound to make good, sensible
Choices.

Another Fall Season

A sudden awareness of golden leaves outside
Commands a second stare
At the result of the sun's delicate touches
Beaming through the air
Providing an early glimpse of some changes
The new season will declare
With the promise to reveal over time
Its captivating flair,
Another fall season that nature's
Designed with care.

The Yellow Balloon

One day while visiting our town's only park,
I was sure I heard the song of a lark.
Immediately my gaze went to the top of a near by tree.
There dangled a big yellow balloon, seemingly beckoning
And waving out to me.
So doing what curious children always do,
I moved closer and closer to get a better view.
Clearly I could see the balloon was tangled in the weeping
Willow.
Anxiously jumping up and down I yelled, "Let it go!
Let it go!"
When that failed, I threw up a couple of small stones,
Only to receive some light bruises and few aching bones.
After a quick recovery, I looked up just in time to see
The big yellow balloon floating by hurriedly,
Being nudged by a strong gust of wind up, up high
Into the open sky.
Today, I still wonder about the big yellow balloon and where
It could possibly be.
I really hope it's flying free and not entangled in another
Weeping willow tree.

Music Tickles My Fancy

Music tickles my fancy,
And it takes me to a place
Beyond the immediate.
Music gives me another
Perspective to embrace,
Positive or negative, it may be.
There is no limit to the influence
Music has on me.
It stirs up my very soul
And inspires me to dream bigger.
And bigger dreams
As my life unfolds in time.
Music tickles my fancy.

What A Situation

Nate dresses hurriedly, anxious to meet his
Buddies for the first day of school.
As he walks quickly toward the bus stop
He feels quite mature and oh__ so cool!
When he reaches a certain spot under a tree
In clear view for his waiting friends to see,
Nate vainly strikes a pose to enhance his profile
Proudly showing off his suave and brand new style.
But what a surprise when water droplets come
Raining down on top of his head and clothes,
With a few drops splattering on the tip of his nose,
Abruptly ending before he can take cover.
But as Nate looks up, he is soon to discover__
With great embarrassment, there has been no rain at all,
Only one tiny gray squirrel answering nature's call!

Let Them Play

Little children love to play.
That's their work for most of
A day.
Not too many things hinder them
Or get in their way.
When they are instructed to do
Anything serious,
Often they become quite
Delirious
Because to them, that's their cue
To play.
Being children, that's just their
Way,
So let those little ones be happy and
Gay.
Let them continue their play.
They will grow up for sure someday
And hopefully abandon the child's
Play!

Moonstruck

Jim, the once popular mayor of our town, boarded
A rocket-ship heading into space,
Expected to return home in a month, in the same
Place.
However, years have passed and there still is no
Sign of him.
Family and friends are now beginning to think
The face in the moon is really that of Jim,
Because his faithful old hound has begun to howl
In that direction at night
'Til the brightness of the moon has vanished totally
Out of his sight.
The prospect of Jim being the man in the moon
Has so intrigued the town
It is in such turmoil and their thinking seems
Upside down.
There is the constant speculation about the moon
Man returning,
So much so, we're all admonished to keep only
The brightest lights burning.
I would really like to think our town has not changed,
But no such luck!
Even the town's name has been changed to the Town
Of Moonstruck.

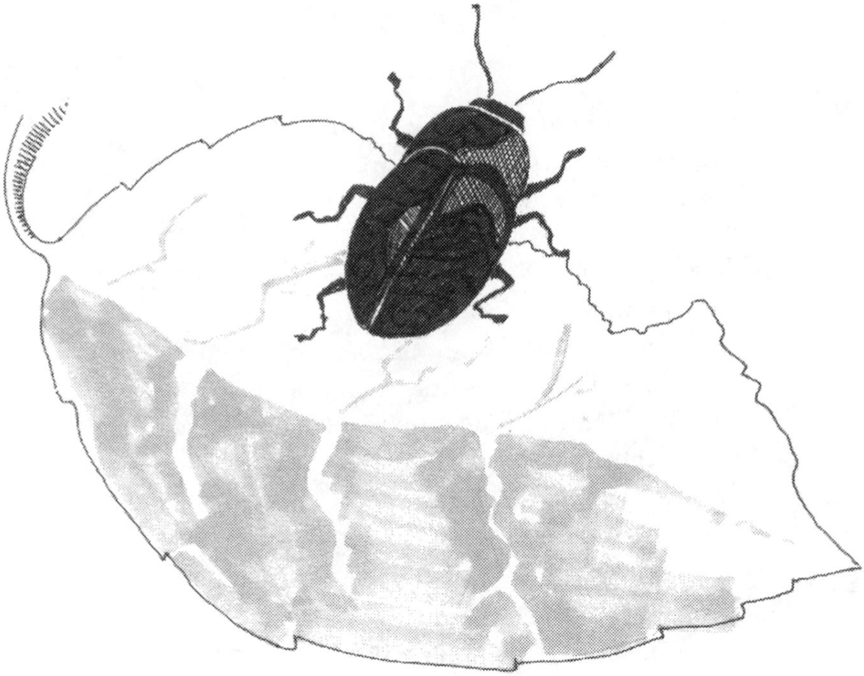

June Bug Days

There's some excitement around our neighborhood today
Now that May is gone and June has found the way,
And a week of June bug mania to look forward to.
We can hardly wait to see beetles swarming down out
Of the blue
To be plucked from the grass on the ground and the leaves
Overhead,
And attached to long thin strands of very strong thread,
Then hoisted up high encouraging the bugs to fly
Zinging and cavorting around about in the sky
Until all is spent by the active events of the day
After which the beetles are released and watched fly
Away,
With high hopes each day after will be as much fun
Or even much more than the very first one.

Couplets

A couplet is a pair of rhyming lines that express a single idea. The lines are usually of the same length and meter. (Idiomatic expressions are used in these rhyming schemes.)

Negotiating through life is like a plunge into a moat,
You are bound to sink if you're not prepared to float.

Any weakness one possesses is their Achilles heel,
Quite often a practice due to a weakness in will.

The one stirring up a hornet's nest
Is most likely the unwanted guest.

If you are told you are skating on thin ice
Don't think you've done something nice.

Remember, judgment can always be found,
But not from every source will it be sound.

Now that you say you are sitting pretty,
You need neither my help nor my pity.

There is nothing like a parent on the warpath
When discovering the child has flunked math.

After gagging on the school's clam chowder
That entire group of students took a powder.

If a certain behavior appears odd to you
Maybe somewhere there's a loose screw.

When old man Flanagan kicked the bucket
He was fishing in the waters off Nantucket.